To Alli

May

God's beautiful creatures make our world ever kinder and gentler.

Namaste,
Craig C. Johnson
2024

A Cat's Eye View of the World:

A Theology According To Puderd

Also by Craig Childress Johnson

Orchids – Harbingers of Hope
Seeing Beyond Easter When It's Still Friday
When Your Soul Itches, Scratch With These
A Second Season of Growth
Travelling Like a King on a Pauper's Budget
Stained Glass: Bits and Pieces of My Life
Gratitude – Daily Doses of God's Abundance
A Second Seas of Growth

Edited by Craig Childress Johnson

Virtual Humor – Laughs From Cyberspace
Virtual Humor II – More Laughs From Cyberspace
Virtual Diamonds – Gems From the Internet
Some Reflections in Late Autumn

Contributor

Summer - First Draft Society
Angels of Mercy – Carol RN
Fall - First Draft Society
Clotheslines – First Draft Society
Charleston Reflections – First Draft Society
Musings – First Draft Society
Americana Medical informatics – Frederick Jones MD
Odyssey – First Draft Society
Voices – First Draft Society
Community – First Draft Society
Townville Sunrise – First Draft Society

A CAT'S EYE VIEW OF THE WORLD

A Theology According To Puderd

Craig Childress Johnson

House of Clement
Anderson, South Carolina

2017

House of Clement
P.O. Box 2404
Anderson, South Carolina 29622

Copyright 1999, 2017
by Craig Childress Johnson

All rights reserved.
This book, or parts thereof, may not
be reproduced in any form without permission.

Printed in United States of America

Book design and photos by Craig Childress Johnson

Front Cover: Craig Childress Johnson
Back Cover: - House of Clement

TO

Those who understand that
dogs have owners and cats have staff

Contents

	Page
Forward	1
A Theology According To Puderd	5
Shake, Rattle, and Roll	7
Offering	10
Productivity Enhancement and Institutional Survival	12
Garage	16
Cat	20
Wake Up, America!	21
Shutters	24
Sanity	27
A Man's Perfect Love	29
Misconceptions	31
Behind Closed Doors	37
Alienation of Affection	43
Progressions	45
Refuge	51
Gray Hair	54

Contents

<u>Page</u>

Sleeping Bag 56

A Better Life 59

The Last Meow 61

A Cat's Eye View of the World: Theology According to Puderd

Foreword

Surely, one of the most delicious of life's simple pleasures is to come into sudden awareness of the purring of a cat, especially if it be a small gray tabby with spots of orange mixed in for genetic good luck. Puderd is rarely more than five feet away from me when I'm at home. Often in the darkness of night I will hear her purring erupt from the mound of bedding we both inhabit for about a third of each day. An inner smile reminds me of what matters most in life - the small gentle things.

During the fourteen years Puderd and I have shared the same house, I have seen five family members die and many dear friends take their last breath and there have been a number of divorces among those friends who didn't die. A number of others have been lost to me because of relational failure. Life can be a pretty gritty experience. It can also be a soft gentle experience filled with hope and happiness. Puderd has been a great teacher in this respect.

I've often said the Lord was having a good day when he invented cats. They prove especially good companions and can't help but invoke a laugh with their antics. For reasons that will remain unknown mysteries to me, Puderd emerges from her feline comatose state every night about 11:30 PM and goes into a truly impressive kinetic mode. I am entranced at how involved and animated a cat can become with a rubber band I have previously taken off a stalk of broccoli. It intrigues me how well an eight-pound animal can simulate the thunder of a herd

A Cat's Eye View of the World: Theology According to Puderd

of horses in full gallop, batting this band throughout the house. I never cease to be amazed at how much pleasure this silly cat gets from my elastic bit of vegetarian refuse. Cats have learned how to derive the greatest pleasure from almost nothing.

Puderd reminds me humans can also have similar experiences, if they want them. One of the great joys of travelling for me has been to see just how fully and richly the poorest of people can live in many parts of the world. In America we seek riches in materialism while other parts of the world have yet to be duped by the consumer myth and still find great contentment and fulfillment in good friends, family, and conversation in the plaza at evening's last light.

In the Old Testament, God used Balaam's donkey to speak to him and protect him from certain grave difficulty. I think here in the Atomic Age God has used a small cat to speak to me many times. I don't hear a voice like Balaam did, but the messages are just as loud. In a complex age fraught with distractions and dangers, we are in need of reminders of those times when we are about to stray into the abyss.

In matters of spiritual life, the noise and incessant chatter of the world can drown out any experience of God. Centuries ago the Israelites were admonished to "be still and know that I am God." This message is even more imperative in our nano-second culture. When we lose sight of God and His voice is lost in the white noise of consumerism, we place ourselves at great risk of experiencing a spiritual declension in our lives.

I hear Puderd telling me spiritual life is found in simplicity and knowledge of God is found in quietness. Contentment is found in good friends, not good products. Trust and safety are really beyond our control and we can only have these if we trust in the One who is in control. "Shake, Rattle, and Roll" reminds me that we all have to trust someone higher for everything in our lives. The American concept of rugged individualism and self-sufficiency is nothing but a myth. It's

A Cat's Eye View of the World: Theology According to Puderd

estimated the food we eat requires the effort of at least ten thousand different people to get it to our kitchens.

Perhaps the most powerful lesson I've learned from Puderd has to deal with hope. In "Offering" I learned circumstances which appear to be absolutely hopeless can, in fact, turn around in miraculous fashion. I've found this to be true for myself facing terminal illness and small birds have also found this to be true when caught in the jaws of a deadly scenario with a cat. We are told in scriptures a sparrow does not fall to the ground unnoticed.

In our warp-nine culture we move faster than the speed of light and often do so impulsively. What looked like a good idea with at least two milliseconds of forethought proves to be a disastrous thing in our lives. Countless doomed marriages, abused children, and financial failures result from impulsive decisions made without seeking wise counsel or the mind of God. In "Garages" Puderd has shown on a feline scale how impetuously running into something can produce a bad outcome. I have been there to bail Puderd out. God can be there to bail us out but he might expect more of us than we do of cats. After all, we were created in His image.

In our competitive high-performance culture, time pressures cause us to start our days on bad footing. We never quite catch up with the demands of the day and this puts us in a highly stressed state. Cats are refractory to this nonsense and immune to time demands. In "Wake Up, America!" Puderd provides a far better strategy for beginning a healthy enjoyable day. And certainly other people will enjoy us more, especially those who have to share the road with us on their morning commutes.

In a world where more families fall apart than stay together, animals can be a source of unconditional love and pleasure. The insanity of the world can be for a season forgotten in the six-part resonation of a six-pack of kittens. "Sanity" reveals how Rebecca deals with the

A Cat's Eye View of the World: Theology According to Puderd

failure of her family. Puderd has certainly been a source of sanity for me.

Many of us have had some severe struggles with relational failures and abusive circumstances. Puderd came from an abusive upbringing and it took years for her to embrace the possibility of life without a tormentor. Many of us still struggle with the idea we might experience life without a tormentor. The Gospel message tells us that

A Cat's Eye View of the World: Theology According to Puderd

A Theology According to Puderd

If we are really honest, we have to confess to having some really absurd silly terms of endearment for our little furry friends and, horror of horrors, our not-so-furry friends, lovers, and soul mates. We would probably be mortified if others ever heard us use these terms in the light of day. Time for a true confession I have a small smoke gray cat that lets me live with her. Somehow the name she had when given to me, Frisky, has been transmuted to Puderd. Don't ask how. I guess it's the same process that transmutes Jan to Fuzzums. Life seems to have its little mysteries.

The important things here are the ecclesiastical merits of this fuzzy spokesfeline for a Higher One. I have attended bible school in Europe and have a letters in theology in one of the Hammermill photocopy paper boxes in my basement. Yet I have gained some deep insights from my small fur coated teacher I never learned from the scholarly men of the United Kingdom.

I have a small chapel in my house in which I keep an antique book cabinet filled with ancient books from prior centuries. I also have an oak table in there on which I have a large plaster Celtic Cross, back lit with a single orange light bulb in one of those little candlestick things you normally see in windows at Christmas, with clear lights in them. An olive wood clad New Testament I got in Jerusalem and the Episcopal Book of common Prayer are there also. There's a nine foot miniature leaf schifellera filling up the remainder of the room.

With my mother having died this week, I find I am going into this room a lot more than I normally do. It seems like a good place to wonder about stuff like the meaning of life, death, illness, dreams, God, the order of the universe. I just discovered last night it to be an exquisite place of learning about the peace of God.

A Cat's Eye View of the World: Theology According to Puderd

It was very late in the evening and I was sitting there on floor, legs crossed, facing Jan (Fuzzums), who was as I. We were having a time of prayer since the angst of the world and issues of mortality seemed much too close for comfort. In the midst of this other worldly time, a very short statured teacher came quietly into our midst, padding so silently in fur lined slippers.

This confident tutor, arranging herself in my legs, gave me a look as if to say "I have an important quiet lesson for you to learn, Watch." I didn't know that cat's legs could go in all these directions at once. This cat managed to assume a position of repose with all four feet somehow intertwined and at the same time pointing to Heaven. This spoke ever so loudly to me, in the silence, of great trust and confidence. This little mentor went quite happily to sleep with a loud purr, proclaiming the peace of God.

The aura of peace, contentment, and serenity that surrounded this small teacher radiated out in ever widening circles. I had a vision of those expanding circles moving out beyond the dim orange light of this sanctuary to enfold an entire troubled world. I even asked out loud if God was making Himself known to me through my cat.

The ancient writings of Faith tell us God spoke through the mouth of a donkey. Perhaps he speaks through cats in the atomic age. I still feel like whispering and tip toeing.

They didn't tell me in Sunday School that God can purr.

A Cat's Eye View of the World: Theology According to Puderd

Shake, Rattle and Roll

The splendid small gray tabby, with blotches of orange that allows me to live with her has come to enjoy the security of a self-made cave in the mountain of blankets I keep on a four-poster bed during the cold cloudy depressing part of the year most of us know as winter. I think we both get a sense of security and safety from hiding under that heap of assorted bedspreads, sheets, blankets, and even old sleeping bags.

I often emerge, shower, and head off for the uncertainties of the work place while Puderd luxuriates in her cozy repose until the spirit moves on her to come forth to sample the offerings of a new day.

One of the things I rather enjoy doing is going to the kitchen at the far end of the house in the morning and shaking the paper bag containing her Friskey's Special Diet. I am amazed at how this contented cat can be sound asleep under eighteen inches of blankets, sleeping bags, bed spreads and sheets at the far end of the house, yet hear this quiet rustling of her bag and instantly be at my feet insisting that I hurry up and get it open.

During the day or evening if I want to find the cat and fail in my mission, I simply go into the kitchen and take out a small round cardboard container containing cat treats and rattle it. It would seem that the treats colliding with the plastic ends create the precise frequency to entice my obscure feline to come out into the open from her still unknown hiding places. In seconds my furry disciple is at my feet, telling me to again hurry.

Puderd has learned small quiet signals can be associated with blessings of different sizes. She's willing to leave the warm cozy safety of her nocturnal repose or the secure anonymity of her secret hiding places and venture out onto a cold tile floor to receive her sustenance for another day. She daily risks leaving her comfort zone. So far she has not been disappointed.

A Cat's Eye View of the World: Theology According to Puderd

It occurs to me a life of faith for cat owners is exactly the same, under ideal circumstances. When we trust God to meet our needs and become silent, we learn to hear His often still small voice which beckons us to receive His blessing.

In the noisy frenetic world we often create for ourselves, we fail to hear His voice and His sustenance for the day is frequently never delivered, because we don't go to the right place to receive it. We fail to come to the kitchen of Heaven and receive His bread and the Water of Life. My cat learned long ago she must come to the kitchen to be fed and watered. Perhaps our cats have something to teach us.

So often in our self-imposed hunger, we seek relief from our cravings in the cauldrons of materialism. The vital minerals and nutrients we need for spiritual life cannot be found in any material thing so we often experience vast deficiencies in our souls. So many angst-torn souls experience little more than living death in our consumer society, victims of malnutrition of the heart. We've come to believe fulfillment and contentment are to be found in mountains of possessions, safety to found in fortresses of financial security. A cultural addiction binds us to the false belief 'just a little more' will finally scratch those unreachable itches in the deepest recesses of our beings.

There seems to a spiritual object lesson in the fact my feline roommate purrs all the time and is in ecstasy when presented with just a small treat rolling across the floor, the name of which escapes me. It seems cats have learned the secret of contentment. They don't continually crave more of anything, just enough. Cats are expert at telling us when they have had enough, be it offerings of food, water, or affection. We don't seem to have yet quite figured out the secret to 'more' might just be found in 'enough.'

Today I sat at the bedside of a dear dear friend who will more than likely never see the sun rise again. It is a dark, foreboding, cold and

A Cat's Eye View of the World: Theology According to Puderd

rainy day and she will probably miss the sunset as well. It is expected Nancy will not survive the night in her battle with cancer. A more elegant, gentle, and kind soul is not to be found on Earth.

Two days ago, just before she slipped into that twilight that comes at life's end, Nancy related to me the vast wealth she has had in the cloud of family, friends, and well wishers who have been accompanying her on the last part of her journey. And there aren't any car dealers, jewelers, or representatives of corporate and retail America among them.

In the still quiet of that death watch there was a very loud message being proclaimed. You might just be able to get the same message from your cat, if you're real still. Wouldn't you rather learn it from your cat early in life than late in life on your death bed? If you chase after the consumer culture's lies there just might not be anyone at your bedside to hear your message. I know. My mom died alone and in stark terror. She chased the mirage in the consumer desert and ran out of water.

> *No one can serve two masters; for either he will hate the one and love the other, or he will hold to one and despise the other. You cannot serve God and mammon. For this reason I say to you, do not be anxious for your life, as to what you shall eat, as to what you shall put on. Is not life more than food, and the body than clothing? Look at the birds of the air, that they do not sow, neither do they reap, nor gather into barns, and yet your heavenly Father feeds them. Are you not worth much more than they? And which of you by being anxious can add a single cubit to his life's span?*

A Cat's Eye View of the World: Theology According to Puderd

Offering

Have you ever been at a point in your life where you feel like you are caught in the jaws of a giant monster and about to move down on the food chain? I recall times when I was absolutely certain there was no way out and I was doomed to some horrible fate. One time I thought it was multiple sclerosis, another time cancer, yet another blindness. A couple of times I've been let go (outsourced) from my job.

Many of us have faced a severe challenge when we were given a grim pronouncement by a physician, plunged into economic free fall when we were told our services were no longer needed, or found a note on the kitchen table telling us our spouse had packed up and left without a forwarding address. Economic and relational uncertainty seem to have become epidemic. Yet, today I don't have multiple sclerosis, cancer, or blindness, and am gainfully employed. I would not have thought that possible at different times, no possibility of it whatever.

Last night about 11 PM I went to the front door to look for the cat and heard a horrible cry from a creature in distress. It certainly didn't sound like any cat I had ever heard. Seconds later my docile gentle feline ran up on the porch, past me into the house, carrying in her mouth the very obvious source of the plaintive tormented call I had just heard.

I quickly turned on the light to find a bird in the jaws of a rather unpleasant scenario. I very quickly removed the cat with bird to the porch and liberated the feathered victim from certain oblivion. Happily, the bird fluttered away, without delay, no doubt with adrenalin maxed out. I never went to vet school; I assume birds have adrenalin for emergency get aways. I quickly tossed the cat into the interior of the house to sulk at her loss. The cat stayed in all night and is under house arrest today. That little sparrow needs a break today.

A Cat's Eye View of the World: Theology According to Puderd

At one point that bird would have seen no possibility for liberation from her captor. I 'happened' to open the door at exactly the right moment just before going to bed and was able to intervene. We humans often face things from which we think there is no possibility of liberation. Yet, prisoners of war in the Hanoi Hilton experienced the wonder of release after eight years. Jews experienced the miracle of emancipation by the Allies. I experienced the magic of not having multiple sclerosis. I get a pay check every other Thursday. There were times when I didn't.

The good part is there is no limit to the possibilities for you. You may be facing cancer or some other horrific circumstance in life. I can't tell you liberation is for certain today. But I can tell you for certain, it is possible for today. If as the Christian scriptures say, "He who counts the sparrows and the hairs on your head will not let you falter" is true and he can move me to liberate a sparrow from the clutches of my house pet, then you can be hopeful that He will liberate you. If not today, then tomorrow, for certain.

Tomorrow you may be flying again.

A Cat's Eye View of the World: Theology According to Puderd

Productivity Enhancement and Institutional Survival

I work in a large hospital, and like many other hospitals, the one I work in is making many attempts to find ways to improve the quality of care while at the same time spending less money on it. Sounds almost like an oxymoron doesn't it? One of the things we as a hospital are doing to achieve this is to implement a facility-wide quality-improvement initiative using a variety of statistical measurement techniques that have been used for years in industrial settings.

We have spent hundreds of thousands of dollars to train more than two thousand employees to various levels of proficiency in the use of Statistical Process Control, all of this to insure institutional survival. You probably know that hundreds of hospitals have been closed over the past ten years because of marginal performance.

A long time ago it was discovered when measurement strategies are put into place in an organization, what is described as the Hawthorne Effect often occurs. Essentially what happens is people will improve their job performance when they think they are being watched by experts; with their clipboards, taking measurements. In one of my former lifetimes, I worked four years as a management industrial engineer in a large hospital and I often saw this occur, especially if I had on my white coat, radiation badge, and acted like I knew what I was doing.

Personnel costs are nearly half the operating budget of most any hospital, probably any business, for that matter. If we 'experts' can find ways to enhance labor productivity then one has a chance of significantly improving financial performance. Yet, one must also realize these 'experts' are not free and tend to run up big laundry bills with their white coats and even bigger dry cleaning bills with their dark business suits. They also tend to want big desks and well decorated offices. It would be an ideal set of circumstances if we

A Cat's Eye View of the World: Theology According to Puderd

could find a way to produce the Hawthorne Effect without the high overhead expenses associated with hiring 'us.'

As often is the case, inspiration came late at night under duress. I was actually doing some homework, at home, for my job as one of those experts. I was slated to begin a training class in the morning to learn a structured approach to interviewing job applicants. As all business gurus know, employee turnover is exceptionally costly and demoralizing. The management experts at the hospital decided to take a stab at reducing this. While being overly responsible about my job, I discovered a way to induce the Hawthorne Effect without experts!

I was lying on the floor, on my stomach, reading through a three-ring binder, struggling greatly to not get up and play a game of Free Cell on my computer or go to bed. While on the edge of consciousness, my eight pound gray with some patches of orange semi-tabby cat hopped up on my back and settled in for the duration. How could I now even think of getting up and playing Free Cell or shirking my responsibility even further by going to bed? I would have heard no end of it and probably been required to sleep alone. No, I must push on with my reading, I thought. After all, I was being watched.

In that instant, vivid revelation came to me. Vision was given. Hope for the financial dilemmas of American healthcare was spawned. In that moment it occurred to me many American hospitals are struggling for survival after only a brief three or four decades of existence at the very same time second hand book shops have existed in Europe for centuries, often passing down through many generations.

How could a multi-million dollar hospital filled with experts be compelled to close while a small home-spun book shop could last what seemed like forever? What was the difference that produced this vast extension of institutional survival? I pondered and there it was, the answer in a single small four letter word: cats. Cats? Of course. How could all of the experts have missed it?

A Cat's Eye View of the World: Theology According to Puderd

Have you ever been in a second-hand book shop in Europe that didn't have a regal striped cat sitting atop the highest book case, watching? The truly productive shops have a second cat, often a white and brown one placed strategically in the window to watch customers, to manipulate them and give them that look that says "If you don't buy a book, my owner (staff) will not be able to afford to go down to the butcher at closing time and buy me scraps for my dinner. Do you want to be responsible for that?" Of course not. No one gets out without buying books. Consequently, bookstores with cats do not have to suffer with non-paying browsers.

I realized in my instant of brilliant insight that every single one of those hospitals that closed had failed to install cats in strategic places to induce the Hawthorne Effect in its labor pool. I mean, if my cat can keep me from Free Cell AND my bed, certainly, a tabby and a brown-and-white, working together, could have saved a hospital from institutional extinction.

Imagine the political coup that would have been for them, saving all those hospitals and reducing the ranks of the unemployed. Even more importantly, think of what we could do with the problem of burgeoning cat populations in the animal shelters of America. We would be certain to win political votes from the animal lovers of America, if instead of gassing cats at the pound, we gave them an important role in reducing the cost of healthcare and saving our hospitals.

I believe the quality of care would also rise markedly. Patients do so much better when in friendly environments reminding them of home. Can you imagine how much better a patient would feel at the sight of a large tabby roaming around under the rungs of chairs in the waiting rooms or sitting up in the window of a patient room, next to the Gloxinia from Aunt Harriet? There's actually an emerging sub-discipline in medicine called pet therapy. It's been proven that by taking pets into nursing homes, patients tend to maintain far better

A Cat's Eye View of the World: Theology According to Puderd

mood and actually show enhanced mobility and physical well-being. One study demonstrated that allowing these patients to care for pets increased their life expectancy! Imagine if Fluff was waiting for us when we came out of surgery. Imagine if we replaced the experts with cats.

Besides, Purina Cat Chow is a whole lot cheaper that experts.

A Cat's Eye View of the World: Theology According to Puderd

Garage

Without fail, whenever I get home, Puderd is waiting for me. She invariably knows whether I will arrive at the front door or come in through the garage. If I elect to show up at the front entrance, which homeowner's almost never use, my loyal feline will often dart right past me into the outer darkness, the nano-second I open the door. Once in a while she will acknowledge me for releasing her, but not often.

When I come into the garage, Puderd always knows this as well. She will wait just inside the door leading into the lower level of the house. Again, if given opportunity, she will dash past me into the cold blackness of the garage as soon as I open the door. It's always seemed uncanny to me she could know the time and place of my return so well. Does my car sound so different than the hundreds of others that pass by my door every day? I don't usually take the Lamborghini to work, instead usually driving the eleven year old Toyota.

It fascinates me how this impulsive cat will always rush out of the warm safety of the house without ever slowing down long enough to assess the outside situation. There are sometimes large feral threats, extreme cold, or even severe storms waiting beyond. When she is lucky, a fine May morning presents itself, but May only comes once a year. More than once, her haste has led Puderd to make some rather poor life choices.

Last evening I arrived home very late on a cold winter night and put the car in the unheated garage. Quite unknown to me, Puderd slipped past me into the cold void of the garage. She is that fast. Her absence was conspicuous during the next thirty minutes or so, given her normal tendency to stick close to me. When ready for bed, I actually went to the garage and called for her. After some years, even cats have to yield a bit of their unpredictability to their keepers. Alas, no answer. I was sleepy. Impatient. That's it. I was going to have that big warm

A Cat's Eye View of the World: Theology According to Puderd

four poster bed all to myself for the entire night. I did. Something for her to think about.

There is much to be learned from the world of nature, even if our contact with it consists of little more than watching the silly antics of our domesticated house pets. One of the most important things for any creature in nature to learn is discernment; when it's OK to come out, when it's safe to eat, when it's safe to play, when it's best to stay put. Such acumen is the difference between life and death millions of times a day for a wide variety of creatures on land and in the sea.

The story is told of how one day Jesus was walking on one of those dry dusty roads in Palestine when He encountered ten outcast lepers. He healed all ten of them. Want to guess how many of them slowed down long enough to even thank him? One. Ten percent. Ten percent will never get you voted MVP in the NBA or even in Little League baseball. NINE of them didn't even give thanks for His ultimate gift. Having leprosy two thousand years ago was worse than death, worse than anything. It meant total rejection, abandonment, disfigurement, vast loneliness, complete total hopelessness. How is it possible radical, impossible, unexpected healing from this vast life shattering scourge did not even merit a small thank you?

The reality is cats and humans are alike in some respects. They often have their own ideas about where they want to go in life and don't even slow down enough to see if their destinations are such a good idea. And for sure, they are not listening to any along the way Who might have life saving advice or even miracles to offer. In their big hurries, humans often leave gratitude and grand possibilities by the way side.

My cat made a choice to spend a long cold dark night in the garage alone instead of buried in the warm safety of a mountain of blankets on the bed. At the time, options seemed to favor the garage. It was normally inaccessible, unfamiliar, and full of dark mystery. The warm

A Cat's Eye View of the World: Theology According to Puderd

bed was familiar, taken for granted. People are even worse than cats about this sort of thing. The truth is those pre-heated blankets sure looked good at 8 AM on this cold winter morning, but only because they were lost to Puderd for a while. As I write, Puderd is wrapped up in them, making up for the sleepless night she chose for herself.

I don't remember many sermons from the thousands I have heard but I do remember part of one from more than twenty years ago in which the minister preached from the Gospel of John. He gave the image of his being on a darkened stage under a single roving spotlight that just barely illuminated the space he was standing on. He knew ahead of time the lamp operator would never move that bright circle of safety to any place of danger. He knew as long as he stayed in the security of the Light, he would not fall into the orchestra pit or through any of the elaborate open trap doors built into the surface of the stage. He could dance freely without fear, but only as long as he stayed in the Light.

The consumer culture sells us myriad false messages about those destinations and things that will satisfy and fulfill. Cruise ship brochures promise us carefree living with nothing but tropical paradise to enjoy. The reality is we all eventually have to get off the boat on Sunday morning. New cars and vast brick houses usually have oppressive, marriage threatening debt attached to them. Yet, as lemmings, most of us chase after these cultural myths of fulfillment at the speed of light and miss many of the truly important things in life. So often the things we miss in our hurry and cravings are of far greater value than those we end up with.

Almost daily I encounter people who fall through the trap doors of consumer society. The media is replete with the stories of people who have had spectacular falls in the material darkness. More American citizens will bankrupt this year that will graduate from college. Home foreclosures are up eight hundred percent in California in six years with one hundred thousand families projected to lose their houses this

A Cat's Eye View of the World: Theology According to Puderd

year alone. Church attendance continues to fall in many regions of the country. It is lower in California than anywhere else.

When I fall, the garage floor is just as cold, hard, and unforgiving independent of whether I park a new Lamborghini or old Toyota on it.

A Cat's Eye View of the World: Theology According to Puderd

Cat

For all but one of my years I have had to make do with one parent as my father died when I was less than a year old. My grandparents died far beyond the dim memories of early childhood. Over the years I have often wondered how it would be to lose my mom, then having no parents or grandparents. At 1:34 AM today I received that fateful call that brought my wondering to an end. I was now on my own, or so I thought.

I have a small gray semi-tabby, with splotches of orange that has been a great soft spot in my life for some eighteen months now. This cat has some idiosyncrasies that make her quite distinctive. Most notable is her immense joy at being held up side down, on her back in one hand, head down, and scratched hard. She stretches grandly in feline catharsis, and yet, I don't recall how I learned of this perverse pleasure. From what I do know of many other cats, holding them upside down in such a manner would put one at high risk for being mauled and soundly rebuked.

As much as my cat likes this kind of attention, one of her other strong quirks is an unfaltering dislike of anyone being near her when she is lying down. Sleeping on the bed has simply not been in the cards for her. Her preference for nocturnal repose this time of year is between two pots of impatiens on the patio, hidden behind a large red gloxinia.

Last night I was lying down, on my back, talking with my brother about Mom's life. In the grim darkness, the cat jumped up on the bed, climbed on my chest and promptly purrclaimed 'I have arrived to provide you comfort and company.' For the remainder of the night that little furry blessing slept with me. Every time I tossed and turned the cat purred quite loudly.

Sometimes God wears a fur coat.

A Cat's Eye View of the World: Theology According to Puderd

Wake Up, America!

Have you ever wondered why Americans are so aggressive and confrontational with each other? Sociologists have explored this issue for decades and come up with little that is truly definitive. Their landmark studies often describe a culture nearly run amok. Rather unsettling reading actually, which the popular press loves to sensationalize.

I think I have found the solution with only minimal experimental research. Like with some other great discoverers, it was not due to a great scientific mind being at work, rather just plain old good luck. Remember the guy that discovered "post-it note" adhesive for 3M and made hundreds of millions of dollars? It was a serendipitous accident. He left a pot full of improperly-made adhesive on a lab counter and the next morning found it didn't stick very well, but well enough to attach 2 x 2 inch squares of yellow paper to most surfaces on the third planet.

I don't expect to make hundreds of millions in cash with my discovery, but perhaps we can save billions as a nation in reduced casualty and medical insurance losses as a result of lower aggression.

This morning, in the quiet serenity of my own bed, the solution to our perplexing social problems presented itself to me. It being Sunday morning, I'd not yet been victimized by a certain strident technology, which allowed me time for relaxed creativity. Americans are well known to be severely sleep deprived. Much has been made of this in the media in the past year. Everything from homicide to excess highway mortality has been attributed to our being in states of partial consciousness. I am among their ranks, at times. This is one of those hapless times.

The past several nights did not find me in quiet repose until 1:30 AM. The emergence of another morning can be especially harsh at such times. But today in my hazy fog I found brilliant clarity.

A Cat's Eye View of the World: Theology According to Puderd

Think back to those times when you have been mid way through some fabulous dream and in the merest instant found yourself blasted into the consciousness of a new day with a pulsating thousand-cycle shrill insult from that tiny plastic monster located strategically near your head. All night long, with those two tiny dots pulsating at one-second intervals, it waited for the most inopportune time to destroy your fantasy. Ever slammed your fist down on the thing in less than a nanosecond in a desperate bid to get back to Shangri-La? To no avail. The transporter coordinates had been lost.

How did you feel when you realized you weren't really in Shangri-La but in your bed on a rainy nasty Monday morning? And it was 8:45 AM and your project presentation scheduled for 9 AM is twenty-two miles away and sixty-three floors up and the express elevators are out for maintenance. Did your demeanor get worse when you remembered you had planned to get up early to get your grand exposition finished up, because you played golf yesterday instead? How was it when those believable rumors of a corporate down-sizing percolated up into your grogginess?

I would suspect that when this not-so pleasant reality was foisted onto you by that digital-display monster, you were off and in the running for a really bad day. I also suspect sociologists could have collected much field information about your aggressive uncivil behavior on the Dan Ryan expressway. Especially, when you cut off that ambulance from County that had the audacity to merge into your lane from the on-ramp as you were attempting to get off. You missed your exit. I think the picture is pretty clear now.

Would you like to rewind and start the day over?

The sun is just making itself known, with an ebony sky giving way to platinum possibilities. A slow gentle rumbling resonates in the depths of your being and barely rises above the horizon of consciousness. What is it? Pondering, curious, you turn over with relaxed grunt.

A Cat's Eye View of the World: Theology According to Puderd

Time slips. It grows louder. Two neurons fire. With minimally functional sentience, you realize the cat is directly under the bed purr claiming the arrival of aureate dawn. You admit to a tiny smile as you lapse back into pleasant slumber

The day blooms vermilion. A gentle prodding politely suggests it's time to embrace the grand opportunity of a new-born day. You turn the other way with serene musings. It persists. You relapse again, searching for Shangri-La. Perhaps it's out there for the finding. A gentle "meow?" breaks your reverie. Nine precious minutes drift by. More firmly now. "Meow." It's eighteen minutes now. With a bit more crescendo, "Meow!" Twenty-seven priceless minutes, more than enough. With total commitment. "MEOW!" My feline guardian walking on my head whispers "You can let me outside now or I can do it right here, right now." I get up, instantly.

With great expectations of the new day, I smile. I don't have to make that frantic dash to that high-pressure high-paying job that enables me to buy all that 'stuff' I will only sell in next year's garage sale. My furry teacher again reminds me of the basics we need for happy contented living. Health, a few good friends, a warm bed, a cat, being let out, and Purina Special Diet.

Puderd goes out to chase squirrels. I go out to chase dreams. Before leaving the house I unplug the alarm clock. I don't think I'll need it any more. I gave my four week notice today.

I drove nice all day.

A Cat's Eye View of the World: Theology According to Puderd

Shutters

Each morning I get up amazed and thankful for another priceless day cast before me to use and invest as I want. Before opening the wooden shutters in my bedroom I often offer a small prayer of thanksgiving for my safe passage through the sometimes precarious darkness of another night.

I frequently play a little game with myself, guessing what the day will look like before opening up to the world. Clear, sunny and warm? Cloudy, rainy, and foreboding? A crystalline wonderland of snow and ice? Today I opened the shutters as usual after my diminutive prayer to find the day before me containing a dark leaden bank of forbidding cloud. It presented an ominous sensibility and I wondered what it would bring to me today. The cat purred a respectful quiet requiem from her cozy cave in a nearby mountain of blankets and other assorted bedding.

Moments later the phone rang. I just learned you were not able to open your shutters this morning, the severe blackness of night had blotted out the light of Hope for you. Or had it?

I recall One who died a horrific death many years ago and how the world suddenly became black as night at the moment of His passing, even though sunset was hours away. Our world was shaken to its foundations by His death and it would seem that even the sun lost a reason to shine. Yet, some hours later, the sun began to give warmth again to the cold despair of humanity.

For many days in spite of the sun's return, His closest friends and followers moped around in darkest despair, wondering if the Son would return as He promised. And He did.

The darkness of Friday yielded to the grand brilliance of Easter Sunday. When Mary went to His tomb to check on His body that

A Cat's Eye View of the World: Theology According to Puderd

fateful morning, she found it empty with the stone seal broken open. She encountered a man she thought to be the gardener and implored him to tell her where the body had been taken. But he wasn't the Gardener and he hadn't taken the body anywhere. He revealed to her that he was, in fact, the risen Son, the reason all the chronicles of humanity are now called his-story.

In that moment when history waited to know if he was just the gardener or if he was the Reason for Hope, Mary learned what all of us now know two millennia later. He wasn't the gardener! There is a reason for hope on the other side of the inky shadows which will one day overcome each of us. He came back from death to tell us he was leaving to prepare a place for us and that if it wasn't true, he would have told us so.

You had your last sunrise yesterday and your shutters are forever closed on this world. Yet, your eyes are now open to the Kingdom in which darkness never descends, where there is no night, a place where the streets are of gold so pure as to be transparent, where the foundation blocks are of precious stones.

For those of us still here wondering what's on the other side of the shutters, we will miss you greatly. Life here can be really scary. Your parents have been through more than most of us can even fathom. I know of those times when the shutters were locked prematurely on the lives of your brother and sister, your brother shot to death in a robbery and your sister literally swallowed up in a sinkhole on the beach while taking a holiday walk. It's more than enough to make me want to hide in the blankets with the cat, suck my thumb, and never come out again.

I often have wondered how your parent's have been able to carry on these years. I wonder how they are going to do this week, and next, and next. In a world where Friday always comes before Sunday, I can only hope they will take great consolation in the promise of the One who said he was going ahead to prepare a place for you.

A Cat's Eye View of the World: Theology According to Puderd

It has been dark and rainy all day but Sonshine is forecast for tomorrow. While we wait, I think I will just sit here and rub my face in Puderd's belly fur. Cats are good listeners.

A Cat's Eye View of the World: Theology According to Puderd

Sanity

I just came back from an international meeting of relief workers where we heard horrors about the many catastrophic humanitarian crises occurring each year in the world. It's estimated some fifty million people are now refugees. The numbers keep rising and one could easily go nuts if the reality of the world's angst was allowed to sink in too far. I just found an antidote to this morbid possibility that's without side effects!

Years ago at a church retreat I came across the concept of passing on warm fuzzies to other people. I have a dear friend who lives 300 miles away and we conduct much of our friendship via fiber optic cable. I have the luxury of living with a truly fine eight pound warm fuzzy. On occasion I will put the mouthpiece of the phone on my cat's stomach and let her purr for thirty seconds or so; a full minute if I am feeling generous and it's after 11 PM when phone rates are cheap.

I can tell at some profound deep level the world is a better place because my cat knows how to purr across a fiber optic network. Maybe I am globalizing, but I know for certain, my friend is better for this great feline ability.

If you started reading from the back, rather than the front as some are inclined to do, then you already know about Rebecca and her seven assorted cats, two parakeets, iridescent green iguana, semi-hairy hamster, and Siamese fighting fish. Yesterday I was accorded the highest level of trust and confidence. Rebecca called me and asked me if I would take care of her various ichthylogical, herpetological, ornithological, and mammalian charges for a whole week while her family went to the beach! I was spell bound with honor.

It was while I was first discharging my important responsibilities to Rebecca's Ark that I had a truly wondrous experience that made all the world's catastrophes fade away, if but for a short time. I had arrived in

A Cat's Eye View of the World: Theology According to Puderd

the gathering darkness to find Priscilla pacing outside, quite hungry and indignant about being separated from her six pack of very thirsty kittens. And yes, they are getting big now at the grand age of seven weeks.

I found lizard food, bird food, fish food, and hamster food and was in route to deliver it in Rebecca's inner sanctum when Priscilla attached herself firmly to my leg, claws and all, and said "Us first!" You know how new mothers can be. I complied and while Priscilla was porking out along with her playful progeny I fed the rest of the animal kingdom.

It was when I came out of Rebecca's Wild Kingdom that I heard the music of true contentment. Priscilla had finished her Tender Vittles and her fluffy brood had had their fill of Kitten Chow and were lined up like English peas in a pod having mother's milk for dessert.

I bent over to partake of this bucolic scene when I heard something I had never ever heard before on my travels in more than thirty countries: a seven-part resonation. Surely, there is nothing in the world like hearing seven contented cats purring at the same time, all wined and dined and bedded down for the night. They were synchronously purrclaiming their happy lot in life.

Perhaps cats can teach us the simplicity of true contentment. In a noisy world a kitten's purr can speak loudly to our soul.

A Cat's Eye View of the World: Theology According to Puderd

A Man's Perfect Love

Nearly all men dream of an idyllic relationship free of harsh words, one where a single pleasing look tells all. Solomon, the wisest man in ancient times told us it's better to live in an attic than to live in a palace with a contentious woman. We men wilt under the power of contentious words. They are death to the soul.

Imagine a relationship in which someone is waiting for you at the door everyday without fail when you get home from work. She asks for nothing in return but a modest bit of affection, more if you are so inclined. Suppose that the whole time not a single ill word ever crosses her lips, instead only pleasing murmurings. Fantasize that she has actually fallen down at your feet and as much said "I'm yours." Sounding more than pretty good isn't it?

I actually come home to such a splendid circumstance every day. Never once have I heard a sarcastic word and never once have I been nagged about taking out the garbage, picking up my socks, or mowing the grass. You must think I am living in a Star Trek Holodeck. To further whet your appetite, I have found someone who doesn't like to shop and has never once asked me for money! What? How is this possible? Isn't it genetically determined that females are born to shop? No, not really. This belief about women is only part of the American folk myth. But what is amazing is that my little lady doesn't mind when I go out and buy some new power tool that I simply gotta have.

And to push the limits of reality she doesn't mind if I bring other women home in the evening!! You must be wondering what my secret is to finding Nirvana this side of heaven? Bet you would pay your life's savings to get in on this wouldn't you? Because you are a dear friend I will tell you my secret.

A Cat's Eye View of the World: Theology According to Puderd

Get a gray female tabby cat and feed her Frisky's Special Diet. Be certain to keep around a couple of those big rubber bands used to tie broccoli stocks together as they make the ultimate cat toy.

The best lovers wear fur coats.

A Cat's Eye View of the World: Theology According to Puderd

Misconceptions

Before getting started, you should know that I like cats, a whole lot. I have lived quite happily with a gray tabby for several years. Childhood was made warm and fuzzy by a fine succession of grand black cats with exotic Middle Eastern names. The one named "Xerxes" got called "Xerox." Another one named "Sisyphus" got transmuted to "Syphilis." Childhood has its mysteries.

Many of us have received greeting cards with colorful emotive artwork showing frolicking cats chasing balls of yarn in front of a fine old brick fireplace or cavorting in some other similarly appealing Rockwellian circumstance. We like to think of cats as a standard of civility, a litmus test of the environment. If cats hang out in the 'hood, then it must be a pretty safe and benign place. Think again!

Environmentalists like to present the natural world as this benevolent gentle space that would live happily ever after if humanity would simply stop reproducing, clear cutting, and emitting toxic waste. In fund raising appeals sent to us on recycled paper, we see heart-rending photos of baby harp seals beaten to death on the ice for their snow-white pelts. Old growth forests are set aside as habitat for the Spotted Owl. Wet lands are given protection to allow shore birds to reproduce.

The natural world in reality is a brutal place where life and death struggles are the order of the day for most species most days of their lives. The natural order is little more than a giant food chain with desperate bids being made continually to avoid ending up on the next lower rung of the culinary pecking order. In the natural world, 'pretty and furry' does not factor into the food equation. Pretty fur is just something that gets caught in the teeth and causes hairballs in predators.

A few days ago a naturalist was pointing out to me that cats are probably the single most efficient family of killers in the whole of the

A Cat's Eye View of the World: Theology According to Puderd

natural order of things. Lions, tigers, panthers, jaguars, lynxes, pumas are all cats which will send out frontal waves of fear into virtually all other creatures who have the misfortune of being anywhere near them at meal time. And most of these cats have no natural enemies and they do get hungry often. The small kitties we keep in our houses? You will see the same thing if you let them out of the house and pay close attention.

When I was five years old we had a huge orange tabby named Raymond that sent forth his own waves of trepidation into the animal kingdom. He had the unsavory habit of going forth to sample the diverse offerings of the mountains that lay just beyond the houses across the street, and then bringing these sacrificial treasures back into our house. Raymond brought us a daily predator's buffet including very large rabbits, exotic birds, rattlesnakes, all manner of rodentia, grass snakes, chipmunks, and other things too lacerated to identify. The fur did fly and it sure wasn't anything that Rockwell would have wanted to paint.

At one time I kept company with a woman who in turn kept company with a large orange tabby named 'Chester.' This sweet mild-mannered house kittie that lounged about in feline contentment was transformed the instant Pat opened the front door. That cat raced out to the nearest phone booth, stripped down, and emerged as Super Predator.

The proof was recklessly and heartlessly plundered from the nearby woods and deposited as an offering every day on the mat outside the door. One best paid attention when going out the door, especially if wearing new shoes that were easily stained by a crimson sacrifice. Many cat owners can recount similar conquests of the animal kingdom by their innocent little Puderds.

So many things in life are just like cats; misconceptions. They are not as they seem. We view cats as cuddly, fuzzy, harmless pets that would do no harm. The fact is they are natural-born killers that kill just for

A Cat's Eye View of the World: Theology According to Puderd

sport. Many of the cultures of the West, and now the East, have bought into another vast misconception; that 'more' means more happiness. More cars, more square footage of house, more closets of clothing and shoes, more power, more money, more RAM, more of everything will translate into more fulfillment, more contentment, more happiness. The natural reality is we get only more angst of soul.

Many of the Pacific Rim nations of Asia and much of Eastern Europe are looking at the American culture as a Holy Grail to be sought out and drunk deeply from. If they can only drink as deeply as we do, so they think, then the desperateness thirstiness of life will be slaked. The rise of consumerism overseas is bringing about an unprecedented transformation of hundreds of diverse cultures and for certain, many of the results are not what would end up on Rockwell's easel.

I have two dear friends living in Wales who have lamented their difficulties with making financial headway in their present circumstances. Like so many others living abroad, they view us Americans as living the good life, the life of Riley, having it all. I tell them, yeah, we do have it all, all right. Divorce, big houses, crime, health clubs, depression, opulent cars, drug addiction, myriad golf courses, loneliness, VCRs, disintegrating families, wide-screen TV, unprecedented bankruptcies, cell phones, insolvent old age, country clubs, and millions of medically uninsured people living the good life.

From a great distance there is an allure, a glitz to the American way that is intoxicating to much of the world. From a distance my dear friends can know I live in a large fourteen room house with only a small cat to compete with in the morning for one of three bathrooms.

What is harder to see at a distance is the vast sense of isolation and loneliness I have often felt in that house over the years in spite of my greatest efforts to fill it with people. My Welsh friends can't see that I have never been invited into my neighbors' houses in twenty years, that I don't even know who lives in them. How many times I have

A Cat's Eye View of the World: Theology According to Puderd

wished I could live in a smaller more compact village, walk to work, have friends nearby instead of spread out over a three-hundred mile radius, know my neighbors.

Fifty years ago the average American house was 950 square feet with a one-car garage. Now, many new garages are larger than the entire typical house of 1950. By any sociological or psychological measures that have been made in the past seven decades, Americans were happier in 1950 with their tiny houses, one black car, and one income than they are in the twenty first century with their vast houses, garages, brightly colored imports, and two incomes.

My artist friends live in a small village where the town center is vibrant, alive, with no vacancy of commercial property. The school is directly off the center of town. One can easily shop, socialize, work, and play without ever getting into a car. Most of my town center is boarded up, with shopping, schools, and social opportunities accessible only by taking a car through a gauntlet of red lights, four lanes, and aggressive drivers afflicted with road rage.

In the United States it's estimated that 68% of all marriages consummated in the later part of the twentieth century will end in divorce. Many of my peers have been married and divorced several times with some having done so seven times. In my own family, my mother married four times, my older brother three times, my only maternal cousin three times. I never gambled on marriage. My mother died alone. I wonder if I will.

A large-scale survey in my county reveals 57% of the population has markers for clinical depression. I spent Thanksgiving in one of the most prosperous of the American states, where the state government does not even bother to collect an income tax. A week after Thanksgiving, an attractive gifted woman I shared turkey and dressing with, committed suicide, depressed over her unrelenting financial problems.

A Cat's Eye View of the World: Theology According to Puderd

The United States is the richest nation on earth yet has the lowest savings rate in the Western World. In the richest nation on earth, which is seven years into an economic miracle, more people will file for bankruptcy this year than will graduate from colleges and universities. A finding published this week shows that the number of children living in poverty in my region of the state has increased by 45% in the past six years.

For the past six years three young children living two houses down from me have spent every night alone. Their mother works as a night teller in a Wal-Mart. The house is disintegrating and if you walk on the deck, you will fall through to the ground twelve feet below. Yet, there is a wide-screen TV, VCR, Nintendo, computer, several stereos, a new car, and virtually nothing saved for retirement. In six years I have never once seen the father.

Chambers of Commerce, Tourist Boards, and the like do not usually paint a realistic view of what life is like in the places they represent. My friends in Wales can't see our collective angst of soul from across the Atlantic. Satellite downloads of American TV sure don't tell the truth. For certain, brokers of consumerism and materialism don't put warnings on their products stating the contents might leave one depressed, lonely, bankrupt, and empty of soul.

King Solomon, who was rather well off, figured out thirty-five centuries ago that 'stuff' doesn't fulfill. *"He who loves money will not be satisfied with money, nor he who loves abundance with its income. This too is vanity."*

Fifteen centuries later another warning was issued, suggesting materialism was a dead-end that did, in fact, often end in spiritual death. Jesus said, *It is harder for a rich man to get to Heaven than it is for a camel to get through the eye of a needle.* There is more commentary in the New Testament about money than about Heaven and Hell. It seems Jesus was suggesting the pursuit of material bounty

A Cat's Eye View of the World: Theology According to Puderd

was itself a distraction from those very things that could provide contentment, fulfillment, happiness, and purpose of life. It seems if material pursuits can keep us from stopping to smell the roses, they will do an even better job of keeping us from pondering matters of eternity which are lost from view in the haze of consumerism.

Why not go down to your local animal shelter and get you a nice tabby cat. It might just be the best investment you ever will make. Most shelters include shots and a bag of food in the deal.

> *For what will a man be profited, if he gains the whole world, and forfeits his soul? Or what will a man give in exchange for his soul? For the Son of Man is going to come in the glory of His Father with His angels; and will then recompense every man according to his deeds.*

A Cat's Eye View of the World: Theology According to Puderd

Behind Closed Doors

There is a rather large regal male Himalayan cat that has been hanging around my house for many months. This huge feline is clearly used to getting his way with the female kitties of the neighborhood. My neighbor's hapless female tabby just delivered a third six-pack of kittens fathered by this rogue. This is important to me because I myself have a small declawed gray with semi-orange blotches tabby which loudly insists on being let outside for short roamings. Fortunately, a surgical intervention will prevent my becoming grandfather to a young troupe of rambunctious Himalayan/tabby hybrids.

My innocent little know-it-all pet will stand at the back door and inundate me with a rather carefully contrived and irritating yowl until I relent and let her out. She knows what's good for her. I don't, she's certain. Be that as it may, I let her out against my better judgment, realizing the only way for her to understand my reluctance to let her out, is to let her out. If the grand stalker is out there, the lesson is learned quickly and kitty is back in the house before I can even think about closing the door. At other times learning is slower to come.

Some time it takes ten minutes or more. The problem is in ten minutes I may have forgotten that Puderd is outside and not hear her proclamations of a lesson well studied. This has on occasion made for some very long and cold contemplation as she spent the whole of the night outside. I may find myself wondering why the cat has not hopped up on the bed during the night, but I don't get up to hunt for her.

When I go to stand in the bathroom first thing in the morning, after one of those nights, doing my business, looking out the window, wanna guess who is precariously perched on the second-floor sill, greeting me with a plaintive heart-rending bid for safety, inner warmth, fresh Purina pellets, and a soft bed?

A Cat's Eye View of the World: Theology According to Puderd

One of the unexplained mysteries of my universe is how that cat can possibly know I am in that bathroom (there are three) at that precise time. You must understand I don't use the bathrooms in a predictable fashion.

An important spiritual principle occurred to me as I let her in the house yesterday after a wandering in the outer darkness, compounded by one of those surprise freezes that aren't supposed to occur because the calendar says it's well into springtime. God knows best. We humans like to think we know what is best for us. We are quite willing to enter into protracted entreaties with God in Heaven to grant us our secret desires. We believe there is something better on the other side of the closed door. Sometimes there is.

Today there was a clear warm spring day on the other side with no feline monsters lurking in the bushes. Yesterday there was darkness beyond AND that Minotaur was out there. I knew this, but Puderd didn't want to trust my judgment on this. It almost got her badly hurt. We often don't want to trust God to know what is on the other side of our doors. We yank knobs. Sometimes we get torn up, very badly at that. Sometimes, we even die.

We often like to say God does not close a door without opening a window. Sometimes God doesn't open the door in the first place. We may ignore the fact it's closed and rip it open only to find an abyss on the other side. Our own momentum may well carry us out into the void. If we are fortunate, we may grab onto the safety chain and avoid freefall. That door may well have been closed for our protection.

Each of us has been created unique with a constellation of life experiences, strengths and weaknesses. What is an abyss for one may be for another an opportunity to test new wings. What for another may be a horror of darkness may be for me an opportunity to see diamonds of possibility glittering in a night sky.

A Cat's Eye View of the World: Theology According to Puderd

Large-scale polls show the number one fear in the United States is speaking before a group of people. People would rather die than be compelled to do this. For me, what others fear even more than death, is a pleasure of the highest order. Today, I spoke before groups twice, relishing every moment, wishing I had a multitude more of them. I could happily stand in a stadium before ten thousand.

Every time I get on an airplane, which I've done hundreds of times, I am amazed most of the people around me quite blithely pop out a novel, the Wall Street Journal, or a lap-top computer and carry on with the ordinary doings of life. Me? I'm too busy leaving my fingerprints in the steel of the armrest to be bothered with something as trivial as reading or pounding on my computer. I don't do well flying, especially in TURBULENCE! I think about nothing except the delicious prospect of that small bounce that comes when the wheels touch down on my beloved terra firma once again.

After going her own way for a season, my cat comes to realize I had a better plan for her. Her animated scamper and gleeful gurgle as she rushes back into my safety tells me she has accomplished some learning. I had offered her security, food, repose. She chose darkness, want, and fear. Alas, the next day she forgets. But, so do we.

Only God knows the future and only God is able to know what is really best for us. Surely if I can see to the best interests of my house pet, then we can trust God to bring the right mix of experiences and challenges to enrich our lives and to grow us past our fears. We can believe He has nothing but our ultimate welfare in mind. After all, we were bought with a Great Price.

The promise of the Christian message is God will withhold no good thing from us. At the same time, He doesn't promise us freedom from turbulence. Yet, we can often seek out the safety of smooth air by

A Cat's Eye View of the World: Theology According to Puderd

following His precepts, including honoring closed doors. And, He will see His chosen through to a safe landing in Heaven.

When God lets us out, He also remembers to let us back in.

> *Now unto him that is able to do exceeding abundantly above all that we ask or think, according to the power that worketh in us.*

A Cat's Eye View of the World: Theology According to Puderd

Alienation of Affection

Last year in North Carolina a woman was awarded $253,000 in a civil judgment against another woman under a rare statute. It seems the defendant had successfully drawn the attentions and affections of a married man away from his wife, effectively disrupting the plaintiff's marriage. In three states it's possible to sue another who has been shown responsible for causing the loss of affection from one's marriage partner. The legislatures of these states have rightfully determined that loss of affection from one's spouse is a serious matter and has allowed for financial recourse under a civil statute called "Alienation of Affection."

There is a fine small college campus near the hospital where I work and for a number of years past I often enjoyed walking on this forested campus with a physician during our lunch hour. We often spoke of finding our personal destinies and gaining self-fulfillment. His enthusiasm grew for this and we shared spirited conversation over the months.

One day my friend seemed especially animated and he let on to me that he had met a woman at a healing conference and was quite taken with her and could communicate with her like no other in the world. He admitted to staying evenings in his office after seeing his last patient and spending extended periods of time on the phone with this distant consort. His state of entrancement grew and I repeatedly warned him that if he continued to have correspondence and calls with her, he would only succeed in destroying his own family and hers. I often said "Don't do it! Doooon't do it!"

He did it. He left the church, sold his practice, left his fine wife, his four children, and all his friends. Next thing we heard he was living in the same state and in the same city from which the defendant hailed. On occasion I cross paths with his ex-wife in the hospital and see on her hollow tear-stained cheeks the clear mark of alienation and

A Cat's Eye View of the World: Theology According to Puderd

abandonment. Unfortunately, in this state the plaintiff has no statutory grounds for an action against the thief who stole her husband's affection and she has been forced to leave her children and home and return to the workplace.

Several years back I watched this same haunting scenario occur under my very own eyes on a daily basis. A devout Christian employee in the hospital left her church, husband, children, job, friends, and home for a profane fellow who boasted of disrupting marriages. When this fellow first came to work in the hospital, Janet had no use whatever for Bill. Yet, he was ultimately able to steal her affection away from her husband and have a son by her. Years later both of these episodes still spook me and I realize in a fallen world how fragile loyalty and affection really are.

For some years now I have rather enjoyed the company of a small gray tabby cat I call Puderd. I mean really enjoyed. There was no other cat in my life and there wasn't going to be, that is until Blondie.

I had not seen my good friend Paula in many months and a few days ago I visited her house. It was there that I encountered the most magnificent, affectionate, attentive, beautiful blond tabby cat one could ever wish for. It was love at first sight.

When I got home later in the day and found Puderd waiting for me, it was different for me, really different. I realized my affection had been stolen by Blondie, that Puderd would have had a case for civil action against me if we had lived in North Carolina, had been human, and we had been married. After all, Blondie was more affectionate, attentive, and attractive than Puderd. Seriously, I was quite amazed at how my affection for my wonderful household pet had been altered so noticeably.

After this small but very real experience with these two cats, it occurred to me that I was no different than my physician friend or my

A Cat's Eye View of the World: Theology According to Puderd

secretary. My affections can be stolen be a friend's cat or a magnificent woman entering my world for the first time. How many times have my vain imaginations about what seems to be the perfect woman stolen all my attentions away from the one I'm with. In fact, this has been enough of an issue as to keep me from having ever married. It seems Paula's cat had unwittingly made an indictment as to my true nature.

As tragic as it is to have a spouse take his affection and give it to another or as painful as it is for a girlfriend to be dumped for another, there is another alienation of affection that is even more devastating with much farther reaching consequences. Taking our affections for God and things of the spirit and giving them to the world can cast us into a vortex of alienation and emptiness that would make a cosmic black hole look inviting by comparison.

The writers of the Old and New Testaments well understood human nature. We can be easily distracted by many things around us and forget our callings as heirs to the Kingdom of God. Like the prodigal son, we want to take the money and run and experience all the glamour the world has to offer. So often we merely end up homeless in a pig pen, bankrupt of soul, eating trodden spoils from the mud. We have traded in the new Cadillac for a broken-down Volkswagen.

The important issue at this point is deciding if we will stay in the pig sty or if we will get up, face home, and start walking. We might just find a warm embrace and warm robe at the end of our long journey, as did that young wanderer thirty five centuries ago. His father understood human nature as does our Father in Heaven. It is to our great good fortune the One who was before the foundations of time has never wavered in His affection for us. He nailed that down for us.

> *Whatever things were gain to me, those things I have counted as loss for the sake of Christ. More than that, I count all things to be loss in view of the surpassing value of*

A Cat's Eye View of the World: Theology According to Puderd

knowing Christ Jesus my Lord, for whom I have suffered the loss of all things, and count them but rubbish in order that I may gain Christ, and may be found in Him, not having a righteousness of my own derived from the law, but that which is through faith in Christ, the righteousness which comes from God on the basis of faith.

A Cat's Eye View of the World: Theology According to Puderd

Progressions

When Puderd came to live with me several years ago, she clearly had some emotional boundary issues. Perhaps, these arose from the fact that in her prior household, a young teenage girl derived great pleasure from harassing and teasing my refugee feline. No doubt, this girl was "kicking the dog" as her father and mother had split up and was now troubled.

The magnitude of Puderd's life challenges is evident from the fact that in the years Puderd has lived with me, she has never once gone back to her former home of four years despite it being less than half a mile away and requiring but crossing one low-risk street.

Soon after Puderd's arrival, I noted she would have nothing to do with getting up on the bed and instead spent her nights in unknown parts of the house. And for certain, she would have nothing whatever to do with girls or women who came to the house. Gradually, my tentative gray tabby progressed to venturing into the bedroom and sleeping in the window or on the floor, but never on the bed. For six months I slept alone.

The night my brother called and told me Mom had just died, Puderd jumped up on the bed, and in the endearing manner that cats do, made a nest and settled in for the duration. I haven't slept alone since.

In the years following, Puderd has made significant progress in recovery. Puderd is now quite happy to be carried around upside down, scratched on her fluffy underside turned topside, and chased at warp nine throughout the house.

In the past two weeks or so I have noticed that, like the migration of tectonic plates, Puderd's nesting site on the bed has been moving south. My feet are at the north end when I am lying on the bed and Puderd has always found the north end by my feet safer than the south

A Cat's Eye View of the World: Theology According to Puderd

end by my head. This week she has actually gotten up near my shoulders a couple of nights. Her head is now within easy scratching range. She's finding that moving south during winter isn't such a bad idea after all.

For many years I have been haunted by a relational progression that takes place among humans. Unlike the endearing ones that I and other humans have had with our cats, this one is rather unsettling and sobering. As cats get attached to their keepers, they develop a sense of safety and will submit to an upside down view of the world, knowing their guardians have their heads on right side up. It has been my observation that as people become more attached to each other, they often become much more at-risk for emotional trauma from their significant others. We have often heard "We most often hurt those we love."

This finally makes sense to me. For those of us raised in abusive and dysfunctional households, a sense of personal security and strong self-esteem became a fleeting mirage in the desert. It took very little for any transient sense of security and positive esteem to be vaporized in the heat of relational conflict. As we have moved into adulthood, many of us have discovered some powerful learning from turbulent early years has remained well entrenched in our psyche, only to re-emerge decades later at the most unexpected times.

We often find a shame-based view of ourselves detonates with no notice; most often when someone we really care about unwittingly punches one of our emotional buttons. What is a new insight for me is an understanding of why it is people we care about most have the fiendish ability to target these and fire away.

Yesterday a very dear friend was relating to me she had purchased some furniture. A casual friend, Jack, helping her move it, had made a comment to the effect, "Have you thought about where you are going to put and use this furniture that you have wasted your money on and

A Cat's Eye View of the World: Theology According to Puderd

consumed my day by asking me to move?" Ellen related she would figure out a place for it and let it go at that. She did not over-react at all.

It occurred to me if I had asked her the same thing in the same tone it would have blown her away. I would have detonated a cascade of shame in her reverberating for days, potentially disrupting our friendship. I know her. I know me. It's not far-fetched to believe we might have been permanently estranged by the errant comment, if I had made it. Ellen agreed if I had made the comment in the same tone it would have been profoundly toxic to her.

What's the difference if I had made it or Jack made it? Here it is. Ellen has no emotional investment in Jack and what he thinks does not have the ability to threaten her tenuous sense of self-esteem or security. On the other hand, Ellen has a lot of emotional investment in me. What I think about her or her actions does have great potential to incinerate her sense of esteem and security.

Furthermore, I have the ability to take something away from her that she highly values: myself. I can in so many words or innuendos tell her she has been a bad little girl and needs to be punished, that her punishment will be abandonment and rejection. And we wonder why people panic, get defensive, and go to Defcon 1 in a nano-second? If you think you are about to lose one of your most cherished possessions, you will scramble faster that the First Airborne Squadron on full alert.

Ellen and I have done this a couple of times. I have done it with others times without number. The problem is defense strategies don't work in relational crises. Resolution of relational challenges requires openness and vulnerability, not force field generators and disrupted communication channels. Defensiveness is plain awful to experience. If you have ever had your genuine efforts at reconciliation rebuffed by someone's force fields, you know this too well.

A Cat's Eye View of the World: Theology According to Puderd

Unfortunately, we learned as children the only way to have a sense of safety was to stay defended at Defcon 1. We learned this so well we failed to realize there can be a peacetime and people can have constructive exchanges and differences without going to war. I have never learned that women can be angry with me and NOT have their hand on the rejection button. I am still trying to figure out anger and rejection don't have to be soul mates.

If I push a button in a shame-based individual (and most of us in the West are such) and she becomes defended and angry, feeling like a naughty child, then I as a shamed-based individual will get the return false message that I have been a bad little boy. I will feel rebuffed, panic, and expect to get that most cruel and unusual punishment, rejection. I better fire first. Want to see a conflict over nothing grow faster than the dandelions in my lawn? Let two shame-based people become emotionally invested in each other and just watch. You won't have to wait long.

Ellen and I have started getting to the place where we can laugh about some of the nonsense we were subjected to as kids. We both learned children were to be seen and not heard, that acceptance was conditional on performance and perfection, that love was conditional, that anger was the prelude to rejection and abandonment. We still believe this to some degree but are beginning to figure out there's another song to sing. And we have discovered we both like to dance.

What I have not fully figured out is a solution to the approach-avoidance conflict that arises within people who are attracted to each other but at the same time are repelled by the recognition of an ever-increasing risk of emotional injury. I've often wondered if it's not better to maintain casual relationships that keep the risk of psychological pain at acceptable levels. I still have not yet gained a grasp of what there is beyond Defcon 1, in experiencing true soul intimacy with others. I suspect that lesson got omitted in my early years. But, I am just now beginning to get the first installments of an

A Cat's Eye View of the World: Theology According to Puderd

education in mid-life suggesting a possible solution to the approach-avoidance conflicts that seems to tyrannize so many of us.

If my self-esteem is conditional on what others think of my performance and state of perfection, then I'm in really big trouble. If I believe love is only a conditional thing, then I will find the love of others tenuous at best. If I believe I'm not granted the right to speak, then the strong words of another will be an indictment without defense. If I believe another person is the keeper of my fortune, fate, and faith, my future fears will come to fruition

If I truly believe my value, dignity, and worth as an individual is a fixed immutable reality in the universe then I needn't fear the words of another will be able to shatter my self-image. If I profoundly believe I'm part of God's perfect family and forever have an eternal place in life, then I needn't fear someone else putting me out in the night emotionally. If a Member of my family has willingly been put to death to spare me an unjust punishment, I can never claim to be ignorant of unconditional love. If I believe I'm an heir to a fortune beyond measure, need I ever fear bankruptcy of soul? Need I ever allow the words of another to cause me to be faint of heart?

Beyond the tortured legalism of organized religion, beyond the tyranny of institutionalized belief systems, beyond the exhausting performance expectations of works-based theologies, beyond the horrors of forty centuries of creed-based abuses, there's a message embedded in the universe that can provide a way out for myself and the Ellens of the world, a realization it's safe to turn off the force-field generators and let others inside our perimeters, to trust Another for true Peace.

> *For since the creation of the world His invisible attributes, His eternal power and divine nature, have been clearly seen, being understood through what has been made ... And not only this, but we also exult in God through our Lord Jesus*

A Cat's Eye View of the World: Theology According to Puderd

Christ, through whom we have now received our reconciliation ... There is therefore now no condemnation for those who are in Christ Jesus ... you have received a spirit of adoption as sons by which we cry out "Abba! Father!" ... The Spirit Himself bears witness with our spirit that we are children of God ... If God is for us, who is against us? He who did not spare His own Son, but delivered Him up for us all, how will He not also with Him freely give us all things?

A Cat's Eye View of the World: Theology According to Puderd

Refuge

This winter, here in the southeast, we have experienced the harsh abuses of the so-called El Nino effect, even though the causative patch of warm Pacific Ocean water is more than seven thousand miles distant. Many of our days have been dark and leaden, battered by intense unrelenting rain and howling winds. Numerous people throughout the country have lost their homes this winter. Some have died. Hundreds of thousand shivered in sub-zero temperatures, sans heat and light.

It is the kind of weather that makes one appreciate the security and comfort of four-poster beds and warm furry foot warmers. I find arising in the dark on such days a special challenge, not made a bit easier by the prospect of leaving a warm cozy nest shared with a splendid feline.

For three years I've enjoyed the constancy of Puderd's unconditional affection. It's my good fortune to live in a time and space where a small gray tabby cat feels sufficient serenity and contentment to greet each day with a sustained purring vibrato. I count my blessings every morning to wake in peace and live out the day in harmony. Many places in the world are in such turmoil and agony that cats have, no doubt, long disappeared from them. Certainly, those few that remain are too busy surviving to purr.

One of my delights in coming home each evening is going into the bedroom to discard my coat, tie, and other trappings of professionalism. This is greatly enhanced when I find my fuzzy pet yet buried in the bedding, seemingly unmoved from ten hours earlier, still making her resonant vibrato. My gray and orange tabby had not given any concern for the likes of food, shelter, or safety during her quiet day of leisure.

A Cat's Eye View of the World: Theology According to Puderd

On those rare occasions when danger looms for Puderd, I quickly intervene. Last week a huge steel-gray feral monster, lurking outside, caught my hapless tabby unaware, and drove her to seek refuge on the second floor sill of the kitchen window. So beset with fear was my howling Puderd, she soiled herself. Launching a brisk counter attack, I compelled Puderd's feline enemy to make a frantic getaway; a flying leap fifteen feet from the deck into space. Puderd was limp with relief. Fetching her from the sill, I could soon feel a rising purr of thanksgiving and gratitude. Carrying her back into the house, her harrowing experience was soon forgotten.

People face things much worse than giant cats the color of blue gun metal; things like bankruptcy, unemployment, the prospect of death, divorce, shame, fear of the future, crime, busyness, competition, the suicide of children, broken dreams. So many of the people around me are in all manner of turbulent white water, collectively experiencing all of these calamities.

My cat can enjoy refuge in my bed every night, secure in the knowledge I will pluck her from feral predators occasionally confronting her. I can enjoy refuge in my bed with Puderd each night, during my days of peace and safety.

But what about when a giant wave of boiling white water slams you onto the rocks and knocks the last breath out of you? Like when a doctor tells you that you are going to die slowly and painfully from a neurological horror. Like when you come home to an empty house and find a note from your wife on the counter telling you she has taken the kids and furniture and moved out-of-state. Like when your accountant calls and tells you the business you have given your life to has failed. Like when your husband is killed by a drunk driver on his way home with your anniversary gift. Like when you are told you are being re-engineered into unemployment, effective at once.

A Cat's Eye View of the World: Theology According to Puderd

Hurricanes cause more destruction than any other type of weather phenomenon because of their vast size and fury. Some of these cyclonic monsters can exceed five hundred miles in diameter. Yet, every single one of these monsters has at its center an eye, a region of complete calm, clear skies, and magical tranquility. The very highest, most destructive winds of horror in a hurricane are to be found immediately adjacent to this oasis of peace.

So it is with the storms of our lives. If we are willing to look for the center of tranquility beyond the fierce turbulence of life, it's *always* there. Hurricanes always have eyes. A refuge of peace is always available to us in the tempests of relational failure, financial ruin, terminal illness, and traumatic loss.

A prominent business man was called in the middle of the night and told his large factory was engulfed in flames. His livelihood burned to the ground despite the best efforts of many engine companies. His response? He laid his weary body down on the ground, pulled his coat over himself and slept soundly, knowing in the morning he would start anew. Beyond the flames of adversity he had found refuge for his soul. Thus it can be with each of us.

> *The Lord is my Shepherd, I shall not want. He makes me lie down in green pastures; He leads me beside quiet waters. He restores my soul; He guides me in the paths of righteousness for His name's sake. Even though I walk in the valley of the shadow of death, I fear no evil; for Thou art with me; Thy rod and Thy staff, they comfort me. Thou dost prepare a table before me in the presence of my enemies; Thou has anointed my head with oil; my cup overflows. Surely goodness and loving kindness will follow me all the days of my life, and I will dwell in the house of the Lord forever.*

A Cat's Eye View of the World: Theology According to Puderd

Gray Hairs

It's hardly worth noting that my gray semi-tabby with orange blotches has gray hairs. That's about as noteworthy as pointing out that blue jays have blue tail feathers. But tonight I noticed for the first time that Puderd has gray hairs; not the kind that make her a gray semi-tabby instead of a Chocolate Point Siamese or a Russian Blue, rather the ones that make her a reminder that life here on earth is really short, especially for cats and middle-aged humans.

As if suddenly seeing her for the first time, I noticed Puderd is looking a little tired, slightly ragged around the cheeks, and a bit gray. Suddenly, the passage of her fourteen years became self-evident. With a measure of disquiet, I realized those same years have passed me by as well. We are both fourteen years closer to the eternal unknown.

Puderd has the grand luxury of ignorance. Cats don't know they have an appointment with death. Sure, they have a powerful urge to survive, but they don't wonder about things like extinction, Heaven, afterlife, eternal judgment, Hell, and dying alone. On the other hand, we cat keepers think about these things, especially during middle age and beyond. This year, funerals seem to have become a monthly affair for me and next year does not promise to be any better. We cat lovers are told it's appointed unto men once to die and then we get a chance at experiencing judgment. I sometimes wish I was as ignorant about these things as my aging feline.

What has been written about Heaven, Paradise, Nirvana, and Eternal Bliss doesn't seem to say anything about cats. It would appear that when Puderd goes, that's it. Nothing else in store for my furry friend. There is a sadness when I think that one day my warm-hearted companion is going to be nothing but cold lifeless organic matter in the ground out back. I can only take consolation in the fact that Puderd got to spend her earthly tenure under warm blankets and enjoy

A Cat's Eye View of the World: Theology According to Puderd

my protection from those semi-feral monster cats that snoop around our house looking for hapless small tabbies.

Inspired writings of St. Paul tell us there are feral monsters of a different sort out there wanting to pilfer our cat keeping souls; with a mission to steal; destroy, and plunder. These aren't furry critters out for a neighborhood romp; rather they are principalities, world forces of darkness, spiritual forces of wickedness seeking to cause us eternal desolation. They would like us to know the definitive coldness of eternal separation from God. The ultimate sadness arises if they succeed.

I know my physical being is going to eventually join my dear cat in the harsh coldness of physical death. The warmth we both enjoy now will dissipate, adding minutely to the entropy of this region of the universe. But the end result for me will be rather different than that of my cat.

In the Book of Life I'm told I can have an infusion of new warmth, life eternal; that I will receive a new body, one forever without gray hairs. Because I do know about death, unlike my cat, and about the Promise of eternal life on the other side, His Hope will propel my soul through the legions of unseen beings that would keep me from entering into His grand promises.

> *For the Lord Himself will descend from Heaven with a shout, with the voice of the archangel, and with the trumpet of God, and the dead in Christ shall rise first.*

A Cat's Eye View of the World: Theology According to Puderd

Sleeping Bag

When my cat teaches me a lesson, I listen. Puderd has been teaching me theology for more than four years now, with most lessons being conducted in early morning. It seems cats are better teachers early on in the day and they have also figgered out humans are more teachable before they get wound up in the frenzy of the day, chasing after all their 'stuff' that really doesn't matter. Puderd would have a field day in a cloistered monastery with its minimal outside distractions.

For years, Puderd has refused to have anything to do with getting under the covers of the bed. Secretly, I have often wished Puderd was like Oscar, the huge orange tabby I once had. In winter, Oscar would always burrow down to the bottom of the covers and pre-heat the bed for me. It was a delicious experience to climb into my bed bare footed and find it lined with warm soft orange tabby fur. Almost as good as a foot rub.

I never have told Puderd that I secretly wish she was like this other grand cat that once was in my life. In fact, I've never even told Puderd there was once another cat. After all, I have to live with her.

During the past several weeks Puderd has taken to spending time under the covers. She has now actually stayed under the covers all night, but just once so far. This proved especially gratifying to me, given that I don't use central heating in my house, even in winter. In January, radiant heating from cats is premium stuff and it's tragic when it simply dissipates into the cold winter air without first heating up my bed.

Just today when I came back from my morning shower I saw one furry foot sticking out from under the pile of bedding. A resonant purring told me that Puderd has had some kind of paradigm shift in her feline brain.

A Cat's Eye View of the World: Theology According to Puderd

In her prior lifetime Puderd had another name and a keeper that often teased her. Our childhood scars often stay with us throughout life and it seems to be so for gray tabby felines as well. Happily, cats and humans are both able to experience growth and move beyond their early fears. Puderd confirmed to me she has learned under my mound of blankets, spreads, and sleeping bags is a warm dark refuge which can make kitties feel safe. She has come to learn taking a small risk and yielding up some element of control can provide her with warmth, pleasure, and contentment.

Humans, especially ones living in North America, have a rather hard time yielding control and feel driven to hang on to it. We feel compelled to be self-sufficient and independent. It's certainly true of this keeper of cats as well. For many years I've avoided marriage because of the control and autonomy that I would be required to give up. It is easy to lose sight of the benefits when all that is seen is the cost and loss of autonomy. If I don't marry, I am not at particular peril and can live a meaningful and rich life. Yet, at another level if I don't give up my desperate hold on self rule and autonomy, I could find myself in very serious spiritual jeopardy.

We were created in God's image and His intent was for us to have fellowship with Him. When we go off on our own self-willed journeys, leaving the covering safety of our Faith and His guidance, we may end up as the prodigal son; living in a pig sty eating corn husks. So often in our own quest for self-sufficiency and control we settle for spiritual corn husks and forfeit the filet mignon that is freely available to us in the Father's house. The prodigal son was often told all his father had would be his one day, but he didn't want to believe it. He was not willing to wait for the truth of this to be borne out in his life.

In the instant-gratification culture of America we believe we have to go out and grab our own fortunes and live it up now. We have lost patience. Instead of fame and fortune we often end up with the corn

A Cat's Eye View of the World: Theology According to Puderd

husks and detritus of alcoholism, drug addictions, HIV, mountains of consumer debt, failed marriages, depression, and bankruptcy of body and soul. More Americans will bankrupt this year than will graduate from all colleges and universities because they are not willing to wait for gratification. More marriages will fail than succeed. Americans now see gambling in its various forms as the fastest way to material abundance. Most state governments now use gambling as part of public policy for revenue enhancement.

The two hundred billion dollars corporate America spends to convince us happiness and fulfillment comes from instant gratification is overpowering. Most of us buy into the message. My cat bought the message that safety and contentment were not to be found under my covers. Like the prodigal, it took her some years to learn of a new reality. The prodigal son finally went home to his father and found a welcoming celebration, signet ring, and robe. My cat finally figured out safety and contentment were to be found under my sleeping bag. I can only hope I will finally figure out true contentment of the soul comes from the Father and His Covering over me, not from the distractions of the consumer culture.

Perhaps if I can get away to a dark quiet place free of distractions I can finally learn of safety and contentment for my soul. Perhaps tonight.

A Cat's Eye View of the World: Theology According to Puderd

A Better Life

I can recall when Puderd first came to live in our house about four years ago I had a modest sense that she was going to be a bit of a bother, perhaps just a bit too much 'maintenance' for my taste. I wondered if getting a cat was really such a good idea. Today it occurs to me that during the past four years I have been far more maintenance than Puderd could have ever been. As it turns out, Puderd has proven to be the lowest maintenance pet possible, with the improbable exception of a pet rock.

It has been truly heartening to watch Puderd overcome the severe traumas of her childhood home. Like so many of us, Puderd's childhood included a good bit of abuse and taunting, ultimately followed by abandonment and rejection for no apparent cause. For four years now Puderd has been growing into her own; gaining confidence in a crowd and a sense of trust, setting aside the skittish fears and skepticism induced by those who really didn't want her anymore. Occasional houseguests even remark on Puderd's progressively greater embrace of a more abundant life. Puderd even freely stretches every fiber of her fuzzy being in feline ecstasy while being held upside down.

I think of the abuse that Jesus had here in His short earthly life. For certain, He could tell Puderd more than a thing or two about abuse, rejection, and abandonment. Like Puderd, Jesus offered only love and affection. In His brief tenure on the third planet, Jesus got the backhand of humanity just as Puderd got it in her childhood and feline adolescence. And plenty of us can relate to humanity's incivility from our own experience.

Clearly my life has become far richer, fuzzier, and more civilized since I have been kept by a cat. Overcoming my sense of the extra effort required to have a cat yielded furry dividends of the highest order.

A Cat's Eye View of the World: Theology According to Puderd

Good pets are so very unconditional in their offers of affection and they ask so little in return.

It occurs to me Jesus has done the exact same thing for us. He trusted His father and stretched every fiber of His being on a splintery Roman cross in order to reach across the troubled gulf between Heaven and Earth. Jesus turned history upside down when He came to earth, knowing the ominous horror-filled Friday that lay before him. Unlike Puderd, Jesus *knew* what lay ahead of him and it sure wasn't fuzzy and pleasant. For certain, in this case ignorance would have been bliss.

We don't know much about what goes on in the minds of cats but we can be fairly sure a conscious fear of death isn't one of the things going on. Puderd does get to bask in ignorance. The price of our sentience includes a perception of linear time and an understanding of an end point for our earthly tenure. It wasn't meant to be so in the beginning. The Father meant for us to live forever. It was our choice early on to go a different way that led to death. It was Jesus' choice to choose a way that led beyond death; His and ours.

Ignorance of eternal choices is anything but bliss. Cats might be able to claim ignorance of the law. I'm not sure I want to stand before the Throne of God one day and claim I didn't know what was going on. After all Puderd has already shown me the simple eternal laws. Love others, expect nothing in return, accept the gift of new life. The result is definitely worth purring about.

> *God demonstrates His own love toward us, in that while we were yet sinners, Christ died for us. For God so loved the world, that He gave His only begotten Son, that whosoever believes in Him should not perish, but have Eternal life.*

A Cat's Eye View of the World: Theology According to Puderd

The Last Meow

We are told God has made Himself known through the handiwork of his creation. We are told his glory is declared in the sunrise. For one who has gotten up in the dark to photograph sunrises, this is believable. For one who has served as the chief of staff for a number of cats, this is most believable.

God uses a variety of messengers to get our attention. It so happens, cats are much more appealing messengers than heart attacks, cancer, divorce, foreign invasions, unemployment, or hurricanes. These furry creatures remind us of the merits of slowing down, way down, taking naps, doing nothing. They remind those of us living frantically in the fast lane, life is often much better lived in the slow lane, or off the road all together.

Calamities have a way of re-ordering our priorities in an instant. When told I was going to be facing down a neurologic nightmare, I found my interest in rental properties, social status, and acquiring ever more stuff unexpectedly waning. Things of eternal significance suddenly became more important. Everything about my life was turned upside down.

There's a tendency to believe if we do all the right things we can avoid all calamity. There seems to be little to suggest that is true. People doing the right things in life find themselves thrown into the frigid waters of failing health. Selfless moral ethical people find themselves facing things of an overwhelming nature.

Life just happens. My theology is not so well developed as to determine if listening to cats as messengers of God will pre-empt some of the big disasters that are part and parcel of being alive and above ground. I'm guessing if we do listen to some of the imperatives about simpler and quieter living cats can give us, I might just dodge a few bullets.

A Cat's Eye View of the World: Theology According to Puderd

Cats are much gentler messengers. I found great joy chasing that silly cat around the house with rubber bands at midnight. I found even greater joy of a numinous origin when my cat had an uncanny ability to understand "presence" was the most important gift in times of great challenge.

When those around me are in the midst of great challenge, perhaps the only thing I can give them of value is a quiet simple "presence." I learned this from a small eight pound gray tabby cat with blotches of orange during my own times of turbulence.

As with very old sages with gray hair living in the Himalaya, my cat seemed to understand what matters and that most of what we think matters doesn't matter at all.

Leave it to a cat to get down to the basics.

The House of Clement is committed to a variety of relief and development efforts including Hospice, Christian education, Amazon conservation, child sponsorship, and travel stipends for relief workers. All profits of all books published by the House of Clement are donated to charity.

Our books are offered with the intent of inspiring readers to living more mindfully and sustainably, to living with a sense of purpose, of living beyond secular consumerism. Authors receive no financial benefit from the sale of these books